I GAVE EVERYTHING BUT A FUCK

I GAVE EVERYTHING

EVERYTHING

BUT A FUCK

HOW TO HACK YOUR MIND, BODY, MONEY, AND SOCIAL LIFE AND GET EVERYTHING YOU WANT IN LIFE

DASANI WAVE

ISBN 978-1-7364482-0-5

Editing by Amy Pattee Colvin
Typesetting by Lucy Holtsnider

The only reason you think you can't do it is because you haven't done it yet.

If you don't find value in this read, prove to me that you read it, and I'll refund you 2x, no questions asked.

CONTENTS

ONE

INTRODUCTION

Beep...Beep...Beep...Beep...Beep! It was six in the morning on a Monday in December in San Francisco, and my alarm clock was going off. As I reached over to hit the snooze button, I thought to myself, "Why am I so tired? I got eight hours of sleep; shouldn't I feel rested?"

As I lay in bed, rubbing my eyes, I was very unhappy about the fact that I had to go to work that morning. I didn't know what I was more unhappy about:

- The fact that I had to chug my piping hot coffee rather than be able to truly enjoy it
- The fact that I had to take a quick, rushed shower rather than a long, relaxing one
- The fact that I had to dress to impress rather than stay in sweats
- The fact that I had to walk to work while dodging homeless people in the icy December wind
- Or the fact that I was probably going to be late to work even though I woke up two hours before I was supposed to be there
- I even told the company that I worked for at the time that

I was commuting from another city just so I could arrive at half-past eight without getting chewed out.

Fun fact: *I was 30 minutes late to that job every single day and was still a top performer.*

I'm sure many, if not all of you, relate to the Monday morning struggle. It tends to repeat itself on Tuesday, Wednesday, Thursday, and Friday too.

While working in Corporate America, I realized that even though I made good money, I felt like I was racing through life— wake up at six, get to work by half-past eight, lunch, gym, dinner, sleep. Rinse and repeat.

On the weekends, I was too exhausted from my work week to pursue any other activities. I didn't understand how other people had so much energy. I felt like I didn't have time to do anything I cared about. I was lost, confused, and unhappy—but hey, at least I made a decent paycheck, right?

Ironically, it seemed that everyone around me pretty much complained about the same struggle. Why are we making good money but have no time to enjoy it, and why do we have to do things that we don't care about at all in order to make good money? Why do we all go to the gym fairly regularly, eat relatively healthy, but are still not proud of the way we look in the mirror? Why do we date who we can, not who we really want? And worst of all, why are we not happy?

The purpose of this book is to motivate YOU, regardless of your age, gender, race, finances, physical or mental limitations, childhood, family, and past-trauma, and show you that you can do literally, (almost) anything. If you're reading this, it's not too late to build the life that you truly want.

HERE'S A LIST OF TRAITS I USED TO HAVE:

Shy—a choice
Insecure—a state of mind
Risk-averse—a choice
Impatient—a choice
Out of shape—mentally and physically
A minority—an internal limitation that I placed on myself
Broke—a state of mind

HERE'S A LIST OF TRAITS I EMBODY NOW:

Confident—a choice and everlasting belief
Secure—a state of mind
Calculated risk-taker—a choice
Patient—a choice
In shape—mentally and physically
A minority—a benefit
Financially independent—a fact

WHAT IT TOOK TO CHANGE
WHO I WAS FOR THE BETTER:

- Hard work and smart work—both are necessary; one is not a replacement for the other
- Trial and error in many different areas
- Calculated, logical decision making and risk-taking
- Surrounding myself with people that wanted what I wanted, had what I wanted, or were willing to do what it took to get there
- Self-belief—what many, simple-minded people would call delusion

- Investing in myself and others—financially, mentally, and physically
- Patience—the hardest part

If you're not willing to do/have/adopt the last seven steps to build the life you want, I suggest you stop reading. If you are willing, please continue. If you're not sure and aren't willing to trust and be led, stop.

I want to start by sharing a little bit about my upbringing. I was blessed with many things by birth and luck, but I also had many limitations and external factors holding me back from my full potential in life.

I grew up in a middle-class family. I was never worried about my next meal; I was provided for by my family, went to a good university, and went on vacation once a year.

My parents got divorced when I was young, and as a result, my life became very chaotic, stressful, anxiety-provoking, and depressive. Below is a summary of the four family figures that most influenced my life.

MOTHER - MENTALLY UNWELL

She battled anxiety, depression, and other mental challenges for several decades and did not receive adequate treatment until very recently.

She was rude and disrespectful if she didn't get what she wanted, and she excelled at laying guilt-trips. She oversteps boundaries, doesn't listen, doesn't process feedback.

Due to the delay in treatment for her mental health issues, my childhood was extremely chaotic, stressful, anxiety-filled, and depress-sing all at the same time. She always claimed she wanted the best for me, but her actions continuously proved the complete opposite. When it mattered, events and actions were nearly always about her, and unfortunately, at my expense.

Examples

She told my coach I was acting up at home. The coach made the whole team run for the entire practice and made me watch—the team hated me for weeks as a result.

I told my mom I was going for a walk. She asked to come with me. I said no because I had only 30 minutes and didn't want to stop and talk to the neighbors or anyone else—she talks too much if you didn't catch that. She said she wouldn't talk to anyone and insisted she come. I said, okay.

As soon as we left the house, she babbled to a neighbor for 20 minutes about why Muslims hate Zoroastrians—two distinct religions in the middle east. She knew the neighbors were Jewish, and in this conversation, she shared that we are Zoroastrian, not Muslim, and used that as justification for why the neighbors should like us. After all, Jews "don't like" Muslims—her words, not mine.

She got kicked out of a basketball game for making the coach's wife feel uncomfortable and "in danger." Later she claimed she never talked to the coach's wife and to this day denies this ever happened.

FATHER - HAPPY

He's truly one of the happiest people I know, but he's negative and pessimistic when it comes to me. He's a person who sees a problem in everything rather than the opportunity. He's risk-averse and thinks all my risks are illogical and stupid regardless of the outcomes that I have attained through them.

He's the pioneer of unsolicited advice regarding subjects he knows nothing about.

Examples

He held a speeding ticket over my head for an entire year—he hasn't stopped—as an illustra-tion of my irresponsibility and inability to make decisions without consulting his advice.

He'll offer entrepreneurial advice, but he's been an employee for the last 25 years and has never had his own business or company.

He'll tell me that I will become sick from intermittent fasting even though intermittent fasting has various health benefits, is advocated in medical journals at top-tier medical schools, and is adopted by many successful everyday people as well as profes-sional athletes.

He'll tell me, to my face, that I'm going to fail and come running back to him whenever I engage in a risky activity, regardless of how conservative or risky it is and what the potential positive outcome could be.

UNCLE (MOTHER'S BROTHER) – SUCCESSFUL, GENEROUS, HELPFUL

He sometimes gives sound advice; other times tries to advise on areas he doesn't know much about. He likes to debate and make bold statements when doing so, but he gets angry if you make bold statements in return. He has a short fuse. He has family challenges of his own and often takes his anger out on other people, including me.

AUNT (MOTHER'S SISTER) — STABLE

She's by far the most stable of the group. She rarely overreacts emotionally and surprises me when she does. She's generous, caring, and kind and has always looked out for my best interests. She's also given me the freedom to make my own decisions and mistakes. However, she is also a self-proclaimed expert in areas where she has little experience.

The summary above is a mere glimpse into my life's influences and by no means a sob story. The purpose of sharing this is to convey how everyone has their unique issues and struggles that other people may or may not relate to. I don't expect you to feel the way I felt on a daily basis in your upbringing, but I wanted you to have a glimpse of my world.

I also want to say that my family has done a lot for me and is loving, but love is not and should not be a replacement for support, respect, or freedom. With that said, I love you.

In the next several chapters, you'll learn why one's past usually determines their future and also why most people do not achieve the majority of the things that they want in life. Instead, they settle or end up living a mediocre life. You'll also learn why that doesn't have to be you and how you can make sure that won't be you.

TWO

THE LOWEST LOWS

Due to my upbringing, I had many beliefs about myself that dictated my thoughts, emotions, and actions daily. Let's refer back to the traits I listed initially and explore the "why" behind them.

WHO I WAS:

Shy

My shyness evolved because my mother embarrassed me daily due to her lack of social calibration, negative attitude, impoliteness, and inability to stop talking. As a result, I didn't want to talk to anyone due to the potential fear of embarrassment that could result. Due to these actions, I lacked a social life, which made me even shyer because I wasn't used to talking to people and struggled to develop that social muscle.

Insecure

All four of the significant family members in my life identified the problem rather than the opportunity in my ideas. They always looked at the negative rather than the positive. As a result, I didn't believe in my ideas, let alone myself. I constantly doubted myself and failed to take action in the areas that I truly cared about.

Risk-averse

In addition to being insecure, I never took risks. I always played it safe. As a result, I struggled to see short-term progress or sustainable, long-term growth.

Impatient

A side effect of not seeing long-term growth was frustration. I was frustrated with my lack of progress in the areas of life that I cared about, so I rushed, made bad decisions, and dug myself bigger holes than I ever thought imaginable.

Out of shape—mentally and physically

Impatience often led to daily negative and plaguing thoughts. I sustained physical injuries resulting from my lack of patience when working out, training, playing sports, etc. Nearly every basketball season, I was injured for several months.

A minority

My ethnicity was something I was insecure about because I thought people looked at me differently—in a negative way—and that certain people would never accept me because of my race, culture, and the way I looked.

Broke

All of the above items contributed to financial instability. For a long time, I held off on starting a business; I rarely made or saved money from jobs, and I didn't invest or build the life I wanted. This outlook on finances perpetuated my negative outlook on life and contributed to a continued downward spiral.

THREE

THE HIGHEST HIGHS

Even with all of these issues, I had a few things going for me that gave me boosts of confidence, self-belief, extroversion, drive, and success in the areas of life that I cared about.

- I was a decent basketball player
- I had a great sense of humor, and people thought I was funny; I was the class clown
- I had people around me who believed in me more than I did myself

I had spurts of excellence. There were times where I was extremely dedicated to my goals and ambitions. I read and studied consistently. I worked hard. I sought advice, guidance, and mentorship.

However, every time I found success, I became extremely arrogant, as if I had proved everyone wrong. As a result, I went through phases where I felt unstoppable, and I made extremely risky, emotional decisions and dug myself right back into the ground. Then the negative cycle of living the above limiting perspectives would continue to repeat itself.

FOUR

WHAT I WAS MISSING

The certain elements that I was missing combined with external factors that were out of my control perpetuated these consistent ups and downs with no consistency.

Arrogance

I used arrogance to compensate for insecurity. I talked a big game but could never back it up. I felt like I always had to prove myself to someone because I wasn't enough as I was. I didn't understand the value of humility.

Embarrassment

My family put me down daily, embarrassed me consistently, and found the negative in everything I said and did. I was living in the wrong environment.

Forgot to think for myself

My thoughts, emotions, and actions were inconsistent, mainly because they weren't my own. I was unstable and unable to build the life I wanted, maintain it, and grow. I had too many cooks spoiling the broth.

— FIVE —

CURE MENTAL ILLNESS, HACK MENTAL WELLNESS

Illness and wellness are two terms that are often thrown around. There are dictionary definitions, and there are influenced definitions.

- Illness is defined as a disease or period of sickness affecting the body or mind.
- Mental illness is defined as a disorder that affects your mood, thinking, and behavior. Examples include depression, anxiety, addictive behaviors, and more.
- Wellness is defined as the state of being in good health, especially as an actively pursued goal.
- Mental Wellness, as defined by the World Health Organization, is "a state of well-being in which the individual realizes

his or her own abilities, can cope with the normal stresses of life, can work productively and fruitfully, and is able to make a contribution to his or her community."

As hard and uncomfortable as it may be, I want you to ask yourself: Based on the above definition, am I mentally-well?

I don't expect you to have a yes or no answer to this question. Many people deal with anxiety, depression, mood swings, addictive behaviors, and get stuck in ruts. Also, many people have legitimate mental illnesses, such as severe depression, bipolar disorder, and more.

Regardless of where you view yourself on this spectrum, you can choose to do many things to help yourself become mentally-well and stay mentally-well consistently throughout your life. Before I share these strategies, I want to share a story that may or may not resonate with you.

I know someone, let's call her Juliette.

She struggles with anxiety and depression and was diagnosed with bipolar disorder several years ago. She has been taking medication(s) for her condition, which has allowed her to remain stable, without severe mood swings and manic episodes.

However, she lives a pretty depressing life. She goes to work, comes home, watches TV, goes to sleep, and does it all over again. She doesn't exercise, have a social life, have real hobbies, or date anyone. She often tells me how she is unhappy with her life and wants to change. She always talks about change but never takes action.

She doesn't go back to her doctors or psychiatrists for re-evaluation. She doesn't find out if she can gradually decrease her medication dosage and create a plan to be medication-free eventually. It's unfortunate because she takes pride in her medication, saying it helps her and keeps her stable.

I also remind her that what she considers stable is relative to the two full-blown manic episodes that she had when she was mixing drugs for several weeks—Adderall and marijuana—which caused her to have the manic episodes in the first place.

Therefore, in reality, the medication keeps her so stable that she cannot take any action in any areas of her life that she cares about. Thus, she stays depressed, struggles with anxiety when dealing with simple tasks and decisions, and as a result, hasn't had any real growth in the past five years.

This story resonates with me because I have had several ups and downs in my life, including severe depressive periods and anxiety issues. I handled winning arrogantly and handled losing poorly. I couldn't stay consistent or stable because I wasn't in touch with my emotions and didn't know how to deal with them.

A psychiatrist who met with me once over Zoom even diagnosed me with cyclothymia—a mood disorder that causes emotional highs and lows—because of the ups and downs I described to her; she even recommended medication to stabilize me.

I was so low at one point that I went to the pharmacy to pick up the medication, but as I stared at the bottle in tears, I couldn't bring myself to take it. I knew this was the last chance to change my life for good before it was too late.

I created a plan. Inevitably I had ups and downs even with that plan, but I eventually succeeded. And I know Juliette can too.

HOW TO HACK MENTAL WELLNESS:

Here are the six strategies that I implemented into my life to hack mental wellness—for me, this meant being truly happy, having inner peace, and living what I consider to be my dream life.

I believe that all of the following will be extremely helpful to you regardless of where you see yourself on the spectrum.

1) The "I Gave Everything but a Fuck" Mindset:

I know, mindset is probably a cliche term that you've heard hundreds of times from dozens of successful gurus on the internet. The reality is, what you think about on a day-to-day, hour-to-hour, and minute-to-minute basis truly does matter. In fact, it matters a lot. In my opinion, here's what a healthy, growth-oriented, successful, and happy person's mindset looks like.

- They see the opportunity before the problem rather than the problem before the opportunity.
- They have an open mind and are curious about things they don't know much about—remember that every expert started as a beginner.
- They think positively, speaking positive things into existence. They rarely think negatively or speak negative things into existence. For example, don't tell yourself that other people don't like you. Don't tell yourself that you don't want to go to work this morning. Don't tell yourself that your job sucks. Don't tell yourself you look like shit. These things are only true and only continue to be true because you continue to tell yourself these things.
- They do not let others' beliefs become their own just because others claim that they want the best for you. A large percentage of people are chronically unhappy because they are constantly trying to fit in with the beliefs, values, morals, and ideologies of their family and friends.
- They do not give up. If you work hard, work smart, and stay

consistent, you probably won't lose. **If you give up, you** will definitely **lose.**

2) The "God is Great" Gratitude Practice:

Wake up every morning and spend five to ten minutes thinking about what is good or great about your life. I used to be terrible at practicing gratitude, which is why I was stuck in a negative feedback loop that plagued me on a day-to-day basis. The result was having less energy, being less productive, and ultimately chronic unhappiness.

Wake up and ask yourself, "What am I thankful for?" I practice this daily by waking up, going for a walk, and saying out loud to myself, "I'm grateful for _____"—fill in the blank with whatever comes to mind. It will most likely feel awkward or fake for the first few days, but eventually, you will start to feel a positive change.

I remember feeling the benefits after four or five days. Gratitude will start to become a natural practice. As a result, you will feel gratitude at random points throughout your day, which will give you more energy, make you more productive, and ultimately make you happier.

Having a gratitude habit in place makes it easier to practice gratitude when things get hard, or you feel anxious, depressed, sad, angry, or any intense emotion.

Gratitude also helps you learn to be humble when you start feeling unstoppable. In turn, you will continue to make sound, logical decisions in your life.

3) You Have to Do Hard Things to Build Self-Worth:

The reality is, the majority of unsuccessful, unhappy people have never really challenged themselves, which is why they don't feel worthy.

They don't have confidence because they've never proved themselves to themselves. The happiest people I know constantly challenge themselves. They fell in love with the challenges and obstacles that they put themselves through because they knew what's possible on the other side.

If you treat everything you do with this attitude, you will realize that doing the hard thing is the right thing, and you will be happy that you did it, regardless of the actual outcome at the time.

Examples:

- In the gym, when you're tired on rep eight and want to quit, push for one or two extra reps.
- When you see that cute boy or girl in the coffee shop, go talk to him or her.
- If you're tired and don't want to read for 20 minutes, but you've told yourself you would read 20 minutes a day, set the timer and do it.

Regardless of the outcome, I guarantee you will feel better if you do the hard thing rather than not.

4) The Compound Effect:

This is the understanding that every little thing matters and will add up—and compound—into both short-term and long-term results. When you look at life that way, you will change the way you make decisions.

Examples:

- I work out even when I'm tired because I know it will contribute to my goal of getting in better shape.
- I pass on that glass of beer with dinner because I know that resisting 300 liquid calories will benefit my health and fitness goals.
- I make that phone call to my customer even when I can put it off until tomorrow because I know doing it today will contribute to the deal closing sooner than later. Even as I write this paragraph at three in the morning on Saturday, yes, I'm tired, but I'm happy because I know I'm one step closer to getting this book to being a best-seller.

5) Exercise and Diet:

Do you struggle to build a consistent diet and exercise routine? If so, I want you to know that you are NOT alone. The majority of people I know do not have a consistent diet and exercise routine. But before I continue, I want you to ask yourself:

When you wake up in the morning and look at yourself in the mirror, are you truly happy with what you see? Do you find yourself attractive? Or do you avoid mirrors because you don't like the way you look?

When you go about your day-to-day life, do you have energy? Or are you barely getting by? Are you tired? Are you too tired to go for a long walk, let alone go to the gym and really sweat?

Do you struggle with migraines, bloating, stomach aches, back pain, joint pain, muscle tightness, or any other chronic body issues that you don't quite understand that just make life a little less enjoyable than it should be?

Fun fact: *in a past life, I made a living by training youth, high school, college, and professional athletes, and everyday people in the areas of functional strength training and visual physique transformation. The three bullet points above are the areas in which my clients and I struggled the most.*

If one or more of the three bullet points above resonate with you, I'd like for you to keep reading. If they don't, feel free to skip this section.

If you're still reading, I have good news. It's actually not *that* hard to:

- Lose weight, tone your abs, and build lean muscle
- Have increased energy and productivity throughout your day
- Live relatively pain-free
- Ultimately be *in love* with the way you look, the way you feel, and the person you are because you know that you did what it took to build your dream physique and reach your functional fitness goals.

Fun fact: *in a past life, I was 20 pounds overweight, was 23 percent body fat, had chronic pain, was exhausted from life, and very unhappy and insecure with the way I looked and felt. **I was the kid that didn't want to take his shirt off regardless if anyone was in the room or not. I avoided mirrors at all costs.***

Nevertheless, after *years* of bullshit excuses, I decided I could no longer continue to let myself suffer. I knew I had to get a trainer because I couldn't do this alone—at least in the beginning.

I went through several bullshit trainers and wasted hundreds of dollars on people who didn't know anything other than the fact that they liked steroids and anger management classes, but I eventually landed a great one who helped me lose 20 pounds, reach 10-12 percent body fat, and have 6-pack abs in a matter of three to four months.

Here's the bottom line, the reality about getting in and staying in shape. It's hard, at least in the beginning, for three to four months. Then after you know what you're doing, it's not very hard. In my opinion and based on my own personal results as well as my clients' results, here's how I like to train.

Intermittent fasting

Yes, I'm sure you've heard this from dozens of gurus as well. The reality is, this is the easiest and most sustainable way to cut fat and gain/maintain muscle simultaneously. If you want to learn *why* this works, feel free to Google it.

Fast for 12-16 hours a day. In other words, stop eating at eight in the evening on Monday, and don't eat till at least eight in the morning on Tuesday. Break your fast with as much protein as possible. I usually do a large portion of red meat or chicken—I don't measure because I don't need to, and neither do you. Rinse and repeat.

Walk or hike daily

This is self-explanatory.

Strength train 2-4x a week

There are certain core exercises that all humans should incorporate into their training sessions, some more relevant to men and some more relevant to women, depending on your goals.

For men, I advocate dumbbell incline bench press—because the upper chest is naturally less developed in most men with respect to other areas of the chest—pull-ups, dumbbell row, hex bar deadlift, and glute/hamstring bridges.

For women, I advocate hex bar deadlift, barbell front squat, single-leg dumbbell RDL, and dumbbell lunges.

For abs, everyone should do planks, side planks, and dead bugs. Google these if you don't know what they are or how to do them properly.

Keep in mind, there are many other ways to get in and stay in shape, but in my experience, the combination of the above items is the easiest way. I'm also not a pro-athlete or bodybuilder shape, nor do I care to be. Achieving that level of condition requires much more than the above.

The framework above is designed for those who want to lose weight or fat, have 6-pack abs, and gain and maintain lean muscle over time—all without worrying about cooking every meal, working out more than 45 minutes three times a week, doing any cardio, and spending much money.

The goal is to look your best while doing the least amount of work possible. If you think it's too good to be true, it's only because you haven't done it yet.

I am no longer accepting clients for personal training; however, I hope the information above can help you reach your goals.

If you feel like you need hands-on personal training, anywhere in the U.S., email dasaniwaveforever@gmail.com with your name, location, budget, and goals, and I will refer you to one of the trainers in my network who can help you accomplish your goals.

6) Therapy

This is going to be the hardest part for many to take action on. I waited until I was 23 years old to start therapy when, in reality, I should have started when I was 15. Therapy changed my life for the better in more ways than I could ever imagine. Here are some of the particular challenges I wanted to address and successfully overcame through therapy:

- Detaching myself from my family's plan for me and building my own identity.
- Becoming emotionally stable
- Letting go of past trauma
- Dealing with anxiety
- Eliminating addictive, plaguing behaviors

This is just on the surface, but therapy has allowed me to explore concepts and ideas with an unbiased professional without fear of judgment.

Remember, your friends and family can give you advice, but do they really know what they're doing? Check out psychologytoday. com to find a therapist that aligns with your needs and goals.

SIX

MYTHS AND MISCONCEPTIONS

I've noticed that most people I meet and interact with have the same common beliefs that hold them back from achieving what they want in life. I've outlined some of these misconceptions below.

MISCONCEPTION #1:
BEING AN ENTREPRENEUR IS BETTER
THAN BEING AN EMPLOYEE

Before I talk about entrepreneurship, I want you to ask yourself:

- Do you like waking up early in the morning just to feel pressured to perform at a job that you don't really care about?
- Do you like how much you're getting paid?
- Do your weekends feel long enough?

- Do you feel like you're able to spend enough time with your family and friends?
- Do you feel like you're given enough credit for what you do at work?
- Do you think you have enough vacation time?
- Do you think retiring at 65 is better than retiring at 35?
- Do you like not being your own boss?

My answers to the above questions clarified why fellow entrepreneurs and I decided to work for ourselves. However, I want to be very clear that being an entrepreneur is not as glamorous as Instagram and your favorite social media stars make it seem.

With that said, I want you to ask yourself:

- Do you want to be able to make your own schedule and actually own your time?
- Do you want to do something that you truly care about?
- Do you want to work *with*, not for, people that are similar to you and want the same things in life as you?
- Do you want to make $100,000, $250,000, $500,000, or even $1,000,000+ annually, but not worry about *when* you're going to get paid next, or when you're going to take your next vacation, or when you're going to retire, simply because you love what you do?
- Do you want to have businesses that eventually run themselves, so you can step away and spend more time with your friends and family?

Fun fact: *one of the biggest reasons for divorce is that one household member spends «too much time at work.» Do you want that to be you?*

If you want the things above, I want you to ask yourself if you *also*:

- Want to wake up early and go to bed late and have less free time than you've ever had before—at least for the first several months of your venture?
- Want to spend one to two hours each day after your day job working on your business instead of drinking, watching TV, or doing other leisure-based activities?
- Want to invest money in yourself and your business instead of clothes, shoes, cars, and other material things?
- Want to spend the weekends working on your business for a few hours each day?
- Are you okay with feeling alone or lonely because very few people will believe in your dreams simply because you haven't given them any reason to yet?
- Are you okay with feeling alone or lonely because the majority of your friends are comfortable with their lifestyles and don't understand yours?
- Are you okay with not being able to sleep some nights because you're thinking about how much work you have to do or wondering when all your hard work will pay off?

Every successful entrepreneur I know had to go through the challenges of the second question before seeing the benefits from the first questions.

As a matter of fact, the questions found in the first section consistently remain asked because those questions are *required* each and every time you start a new project or venture. Serial entrepreneurs often find themselves addicted to this process.

With all this being said, it's important to understand that having a stable job and progressive career has many, many benefits. In a later chapter titled *Money & Time*, I plan on talking more about the best jobs and careers that are not only beneficial for the time being but can help you fund your entrepreneurial goals if that's a route you want to take.

MISCONCEPTION # 2:
BEING RICH, FAMOUS, GOOD LOOKING, AND FIT WILL GET YOU GIRLS

*Disclaimer: This section may be more relevant to the boys that are reading, but I encourage both boys and girls to read it anyway.

Now before I talk about men, women, boys, girls, attraction, sex, love, etc., I want you to ask yourself:

- When was the last time you saw a girl that you really wanted to talk to? She could have been on the street, in the gym, at the coffee shop, in an uber, at a bar, at a social gathering, or even at work, but you couldn't muster up the courage to go talk to her because you were afraid of rejection or afraid of coming off as weird or disrespectful?
- When was the last time you saw a girl that you really wanted to talk to but simply didn't know what to say or weren't confident in what you were going to say, or maybe your mind went completely blank, and you froze up?
- When was the last time you got frustrated with yourself for either of the two challenges above?
- When was the last time you were having a conversation with a girl, and then out of nowhere, she randomly lost interest and left?
- When was the last time a girl told you she thinks you two are "better off as friends?"
- When was the last time you thought a girl was so far out of your league that it would be *pointless* to go talk to her?

- When was the last time you felt like you dated someone that you really wanted to date, or were in an *amazing* relationship, as opposed to just settling for whatever comes your way?

After interviewing and conversing with hundreds, possibly even thousands of men, I realized that these were the most common male challenges in the 21st-century dating scene.

I realized that most men do not understand what women truly like and want, and therefore, focus on the wrong things based on what they think they know is true from the media and what their friends or peers tell them.

For example, most men that I've spoken to think:

- Money/fame matters the *most*
- Looks matter a lot
- Being in shape matters a lot

And as a result, they focus exclusively on these things with hopes to be able to attract and date the most attractive women.

Now here's the truth:

- Money and Fame do matter
- Looks do matter
- Being in shape does help

But none of these are *as important as you think*. In fact, most men I know that are handsome and in excellent shape don't get many girls, let alone the most attractive ones. Even the majority of rich and wealthy guys don't do well with women.

The *most important* factor is your ability to attract and engage a girl mentally, and most men do not understand how to do this; this ideology is also referred to as *game* in pop culture.

Fun fact: *women have their own game too.*

Now before I go on, I want to say that the purpose of this section is *not* to teach you how to attract women for the wrong reasons. Instead, this section will educate you on what women actually care about so that you can learn how to attract, date, and have relations with the women that you truly want in your life—whether that's casually, a long-term relationship, or even your future wife and mother of your kids.

With that said, I hope no women are offended by what I've said so far or what I'm about to say, but at the same time, I give everything but a fuck; I'm here to help those that want to be helped.

With that said, when was the last time you saw an incredibly unattractive and unsuccessful guy with a super-hot, cool girlfriend and wondered to yourself, "What the *fuck* is going on here?"

Don't worry; I used to wonder the same thing too. It's time I tell you what women truly want, are attracted to, and care about.

Women want:

- A man who wants her but doesn't need her
- A man who is in her league or slightly above her league, but not too far out of her league where she knows she can't truly have him
- A man who doesn't put her on a pedestal and treat her like she's everything in the world to him, at least not at first
- A man who can spark and maintain an emotional connection between him and her by saying the right things and looking at and touching her the right ways
- A man who doesn't qualify or try too hard to prove himself to her

- A man who creates a narrative or story about the two of them that she can be proud of

At the end of the day, a woman just wants to be gamed the way *she* wants to be gamed. If you can learn how to do this, you will, without a doubt, build a successful, happy, and fulfilling dating life the same way I have.

How can you learn to build the dating life of your dreams?

1. 1. Subscribe to **OnlyFans.com/DasaniWaveVerified**

2. 2. Use coupon code **DasaniWaveForever** for 50% off your subscription.

3. 3. Listen, take notes, and apply what you learn. Stay consistent, ask questions when appropriate, and most importantly, don't give up. If you do these things, I promise you will be successful.

Dear Boys and Girls,

I chose OnlyFans because I wanted to give away the game for an affordable price and help all of my peers long-term, day after day, week after week, month after month.

Ladies, I invite you to join as well, as I will be talking about the female side of the game and what you can do to attract and keep the men you want in your life instead of settling for whoever slides in your D.M.'s.

Respectfully Rude,

Dasani

MISCONCEPTION #3:
ALWAYS FOLLOW YOUR PASSION

Most people think they are naturally passionate about things when, in reality, this usually isn't true.

For example, I started playing basketball in third grade and absolutely hated it. Then after several months of hard work and consistent training, I began to improve. That's when I started to enjoy it. Then after a year or two, I was one of the best players in my school. That's when I truly became passionate about basketball.

Now, because the majority of people are often most open-minded when they are children, they develop certain passions and build their lives around them. The majority of these passions are things that have a very low chance of producing any income--sports, music, dance, things that resonate with us as children. And there's nothing wrong with that.

For the longest time, I wanted to be a basketball coach and even a talent manager for rappers. I was *set* on these careers. However, I didn't realize that the only reason I was passionate about these things is that I had developed a passion for sports and rap music at an early age, and my life revolved around those things for years. The downside was that I hadn't taken the time to explore anything else, so I didn't know what *else* I was passionate about—yet.

How to develop passion for something:

Try something. Anything. It doesn't matter what it is.

- Learn as much as you can about it, even if you have no interest.
- Fail over and over again.

- Improve slowly over time. As you become more interested and put more effort, naturally you will improve.
- Get better. Keep getting better.
- Become great. Now you'll be passionate.

My goal in life was to become passionate about things that make sense for *me*. I thought about what I wanted in life and what things would get me there. Here's the list I made:

- My goal in business is to be able to step away from my business eventually.
- My goal in business is to be able to work from anywhere, at any time.
- My goal in business is to make six to seven figures a year, after taxes.
- I want to influence and help thousands, if not millions, of people. My true friends, my true family, and even people I don't know.
- I want the mother of my children to have the same mental, spiritual, emotional, physical, and sexual vibe that I have. I want to be with someone who is an outstanding communicator. I want to be with someone who doesn't want to argue but wants to have open conversations. I want to be with someone who will eventually know everything about me, and someone I can trust with anything and everything and never question that. I want to be with someone who cares about me and others the way I do about her and others. I want to be with someone who wants to see me win. I want a cat and a dog, and two kids at least. **If you're reading this, we can compromise on that last part.**
- I want to surround myself with people that have the same qualities as #5, but in the context of friendship and business.

- I want to look back at my life when I'm old and say that I have no regrets. I did it my way, and it worked.

There was a point in my life where I was so depressed that I was nearly suicidal. This was when I created my first list and followed the step-by-step process above to become passionate about what would lead to that list's completion and, in turn, helping me achieve what I wanted in life.

I became passionate about business models that could be automated and operated from anywhere. I became passionate about businesses that could generate six- and seven-figure numbers regularly. I became passionate about communication, psychology, network-ing, friendships, and relationships, and the skill sets needed to connect with the highest caliber people in the world. Due to developing that skillset, I've met and built relationships with many outstanding men and women, and I am grateful for all of them.

I'd like for you to create your own list and then ask yourself how you can turn that list into reality. Once you've made your list, take steps to become passionate about those things via the suggestions listed above. You will thank yourself later.

— SEVEN —

MONEY & TIME

When it comes to money, I want you to ask yourself:

- Are you happy with the amount you're getting paid?
- Do you have enough time to use that money on things that you care about?

If you answered no to either of those questions, keep reading.

*Disclaimer: Making money is hard. However, once you put in the leg work to have the right models and systems in place, things get easier.

Here are my three golden rules when it comes to making money:

- Making money takes both hard work and smart work
- "Scared money don't make none" – Nipsey Hussle
- If it's too good to be true, it may be, but it also may not be. **Read that again.**

In my opinion and experience, it's important to make more than enough money while still having enough time to enjoy life and spend time with the people you care about.

CHOOSE THE RIGHT JOB

Choose a "job" that allows you to either have *more* freedom than most jobs, meet the right people, and of course, pay the bills and support your lifestyle. Here are some of my favorite options.

Tech Sales

The tech industry may seem scary, unknown, or uninteresting to you, and that may just be because you don't know much about it. The human brain has a natural tendency to fear the unknown and stay away from it. We have to reprogram ourselves to do the opposite.

The tech industry generally has high base salaries, good commission plans, inclusive culture, and an excellent work-life balance. Other industries tend to have lower base salaries, longer hours, and require you to physically go to client's offices. In tech, you can close a million-dollar deal from your phone.

You'll make money, learn a lot, enjoy it, and rise within the industry if you work hard, pay attention, and stay consistent. You also won't work day and night, so you can enjoy the money you make. You don't need a college degree or experience to get an entry-level tech sales job.

Bartender or Bottle Service

You'll make good money, network, and meet a lot of people. The more upscale the bar or club, the more successful people you'll meet.

Food Delivery

Instacart, Doordash, etc., all pay well and let you pick your own hours. Best of all, there's no one looking over your shoulder when you do your job.

Work at a Luxury Store or Gym

Get a job at a designer retailer like Louis Vuitton, Cartier, etc., or a gym like Equinox. You'll meet a lot of successful people and have the opportunity to connect with them.

Electrician

Pays well, pick your own hours.

Logistics

Logistics, warehouse, and com-mercial driving jobs pay well and are relatively stress-free.

Massage Therapist

Get certified, work for a company to learn the ropes, then go private, and take your clients with you. Work when you want, charge what you want.

House Sitter

Chill in a rich person's house and make money doing damn near nothing. Work on your own business while you do it—they're not there, so they can't dictate your time.

Apprenticeship/Internship/Assistant

Find a public figure or celebrity you look up to and give them a reason to hire you. If not, offer to work for them for free and work your way up. I know several assistants that make six figures.

BE A BROKER

A broker is defined as "arranging or negotiating a settlement, deal or plan." Essentially you connect two people—a seller and a buyer—and collect a broker fee for the introduction. You can do this in various industries.

I make good money with this model because it doesn't cost me any money. I invest my time, maintain my power between the buying and selling party, and collect a fee over and over again as they continue to work together.

INVEST

Ah, investing. Most people think they don't have enough money to invest or don't know how to invest small amounts of money yet still turn a profit. If you feel like this is you, that's okay. Here are some of my favorite investment strategies.

Day Trading (Quick Gains)

Yes, I know you probably don't know how to do this. That's okay; neither do I! Find someone that is an expert at this, build trust with them, and offer them an incentive to trade your money in the market. Most people think this is illegal, but the SEC1 has a friends and family rule that legally allows this to happen. Feel free to Google this for yourself.

---

1 SEC = The U.S. Securities and Exchange Commission is a large independent agency of the United States federal government that was created following the stock market crash in the 1920s to protect investors and the national banking system.

Mutual and Index Funds (Long-Term Growth)

Investing in the S&P 500 and other mutual and index funds will allow you to make six to ten percent on your money year after year, based on data from the past 30 years. This may not seem like a lot, but it adds up. More importantly, you don't have to think about this investment. Set it and forget it. Live your life. Also, Google compound interest so you can understand the gains potential here.

Real Estate

Invest in real estate portfolios the same way you would invest in stocks. **Check out Fundrise.com. Or, if you have $20,000+ and want to invest in a rental property with a tenant and one-year lease already in place for guaranteed cash flow on day one, email dasaniwaveforever@gmail.com with your name, screenshot of your bank account with $20,000+, and the message, «I want a rental property with 15% ROI so I can stop trading time for money."**

Drop shipping

A great business model that has the potential to make six and even seven figures with very little overhead; meaning, the cost of running the business is very low with respect to other business models. Plus, everything is online, so you can run your business from anywhere.

How you can learn how to make money through these avenues and beyond:

1. Subscribe to **OnlyFans.com/DasaniWaveVerified**

2. Use coupon code DasaniWaveForever for 50% off your subscription.

3. Listen, take notes, and apply what you learn. Stay consistent, ask questions when appropriate, and most importantly, don't give up. If you do these things, I promise you will be successful—yes, I will be talking about jobs, careers, business, entrepreneurship, money, finances, credit, stocks, real estate, drop shipping, brokerage, fast money, and long-term wealth, all on my OnlyFans as well).

— EIGHT —

MY 13 COMMANDMENTS

The 13 commandments below have allowed me to cure mental illness, hack mental wellness, and accomplish (almost) everything I've ever wanted. Most importantly, living life this way makes me happy, and I believe these things can help you be happier too.

1. Don't let your past determine your present and future.
2. Think big, but not too big. Try to have your decisions align with this mindset.
3. Be confident, show off if you want, but remember to remain humble. Don't ever become unstoppable.
4. Be skeptical, but don't be an idiot. Some risks are worth taking.
5. Narrow your influence. Seek advice only from experts in the area where you're looking for advice. In other words,

don't ask your parents for entrepreneurial advice if they've been employees their entire lives.

6. Competition and comparison are the enemies of happiness. Try not to compare yourself to others or try to compete with the next man or woman. Be the best you and everything you want will come.

7. Think logically and take action. Don't wait for the perfect time to do something. The perfect time doesn't exist.

8. If you're anxious, visualize the worst thing that can happen. If you can handle the worst thing that can happen, turn that anxiety into excitement, and do the thing that's making you anxious. If your anxiety is making you depressed, practice gratitude. Rinse and repeat. You'll feel better.

9. Don't care what others think. If others hate what you're doing, it's probably because they want what you have or are simply unhappy with their own lives. They feed themselves negative energy on a daily basis, and that negative energy is projected onto you. Also, no one ever knows your full story. They just know what you told them. Listen to yourself first; you know more.

10. If someone is making you work too hard for them, they usually aren't worth chasing. Also, if you're chasing, they're probably running. Don't run after them.

11. Being politically correct usually doesn't get you far. The majority of the top performers I know in every industry are all pretty outlandish. On the contrary, the majority of people I know that play politics and don't choose sides are, for the most part, nowhere. To sum it up, be unapologetically yourself. The unfiltered you usually wins every time.

12. The morals and values of your family and friends don't have to be your own. **Be whoever the fuck you want to**

be. Also, if your family and friends are subjecting you to an unhealthy, toxic, and/or negative environment or forcibly trying to make you value the same things as they do, do anything and everything you can to leave that environment.

13. Risk assessment. Don't take risks you cannot come back from or ones where the potential loss is too big to recover from. For example, don't invest your entire savings in a company that may not succeed. Instead, invest a fifth of your savings in a risky investment so you will still be able to pay your bills whether or not you win.

— NINE —

BOOKS YOU SHOULD READ

The following shortlist of books changed my life and expanded upon my 13 commandments.

- *The Magic of Thinking Big* by David J. Schwartz
- *The Hypomanic Edge* by John D. Gartner
- *How to Win Friends & Influence People* by Dale Carnegie
- *Rich Dad Poor Dad* by Robert T. Kiyosaki
- *The Compound Effect* by Darren Hardy
- *Don't Eat the Marshmallow Yet* by Joachim de Posada
- *Unfu*k Yourself* by Gary John Bishop

— TEN —

OUTRO

I kept this book short and sweet because I don't like to complicate things. I hope you found value in the read. Before you go, remember to:

1. Follow **@DasaniWave** and **@DasaniDaily** on Instagram.
2. Subscribe to **OnlyFans.com/ DasaniWaveVerified**
3. Use coupon code DasaniWaveForever for 50% off your subscription.
4. Listen, take notes, and apply what you learn. Stay consistent, ask questions when appropriate, and most importantly, don't give up. If you do these things, I promise you will be successful.

Lastly, remember that when it's all said and done, you're just like me, and I'm just like you. You can accomplish whatever you put your mind to. My goal is to make you as happy, successful, and fulfilled as possible.

When in doubt, Give Everything but a Fuck.

Love,

Dasani Wave

ACKNOWLEDGMENTS

Everybody knows what role they played.

ABOUT THE AUTHOR

Dasani Wave is a consultant, coach, mentor, serial entrepreneur, and investor specializing in helping others attain what they want in life. He is passionate about business, human and social psychology, and communication. He promotes a growth mindset rather than a fixed one; he believes that happiness is dependent on you, not dependent on what is around you.

I Gave Everything but a Fuck,

Dasani

Business Instagram: **@DasaniDaily**
Personal Instagram: **@DasaniWave**
Website: **DasaniWave.com**

www.ingramcontent.com/pod-product-compliance
Lightning Source LLC
Chambersburg PA
CBHW020607030426
42337CB00013B/1264